THE FINAL GOODBYE TO
KILIMANJARO.

CONTENTS

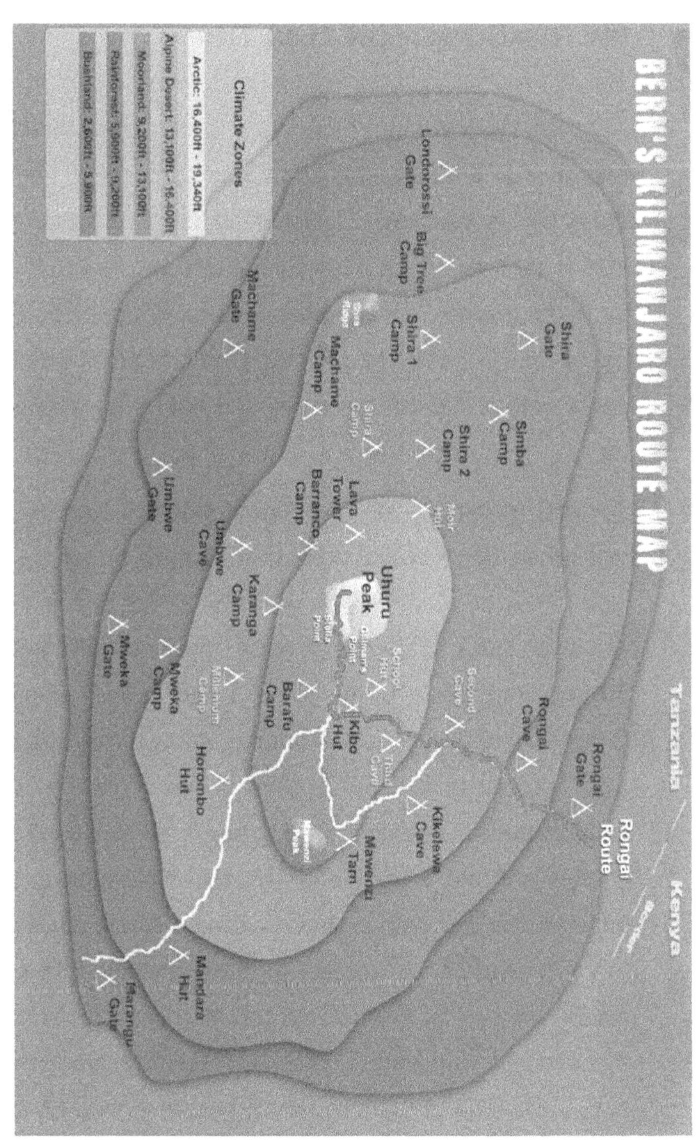

BERN'S KILIMANJARO ROUTE MAP
Tanzania
Kenya
Border
Rongai Route
Rongai Gate
Rongai Cave
Shira Gate
Simba Camp
Shira 2 Camp
Moir Hut
Second Cave
Kikelewa Cave
Londorossi Gate
Big Tree Camp
Shira 1 Camp
Uhuru Peak
School Hut
Third Cave
Shira Camp
Lava Tower
Gillman's Point
Kibo Hut
Mawenzi Tarn
Shira Ridge
Machame Camp
Barranco Camp
Stella Point
Mawenzi Peak
Barafu Camp
Machame Gate
Karanga Camp
Umbwe Cave
Millenium Camp
Horombo Hut
Mandara Hut
Umbwe Gate
Mweka Camp
Mweka Gate
Marangu Gate
Climate Zones
Arctic: 16,400ft - 19,340ft
Alpine Desert: 13,100ft - 16,400ft
Moorland: 9,200ft - 13,100ft
Rainforest: 5,900ft - 9,200ft
Bushland: 2,600ft - 5,900ft

MY REASONS FOR THIS TRIP

After the 2005 trip that I saw as a failure, even though the response to the television show was so positive, I felt as if there was something unfinished in my life. It didn't help that every time I did a motivational talk people would come up to me and say 'Ah shame you were so close you should try again', but they forgot that I had been successful 2 years before that but the press had not really followed the trip.

So after giving it a lot of thought I decided to give it one last go so that I could close that chapter of my life on a high. I decided that if I was going to do this one last time I would go back to tried and tested methods of training in the mountains and in the gym. I had been training with Cindy for about a year and if anyone knew me, she did. I also decided to ask her to join me as a member of my support team. A couple weeks later I did some talks at a church in Pretoria, and after an extremely long day with four talks in one day, a student named Nadia came up to me and asked if she could join the expedition. This gave me an idea to let people join us, at a cost, as a form of motivational workshop. The idea seemed great initially, but by the time of the trip, only 3 people signed on for the trip.

One of the companies also came up with the idea of using technology to track and publicy your progress on the mountain. We did this by putting a GPS tracking device on my wheelchair so that people could see where we are by viewing it on a map from my website. They also gave us the capability to upload daily video clips from the mountain to my website. The third thing we did to encourage people to participate in our climb was to give them the opportunity to send us text from their mobile phones. If only we had this technology for my first climb. We would also take a new make of laptop up the mountain to enable us to communicate with the outside world. I was a bit nervous of this because the last laptop we had taken up had crashed, with our entire collection of photo's and recordings on, just before we had completed the descent.

THE BUILD UP

Over the next couple of months it was a real rollercoaster of successes and failures. My training was reaching new heights with being able to continually train in the gym for 8 hours per day and on weekends climbing very steep, rocky mountains in record time. However, at the same time the people and companies that had shown a lot of excitement about being part of the trip were slowly withdrawing one by one. Eventually leaving four people, Paul, Nadia, Neil and Johan K, to join us on the trip. This was of course in addition to my support team which consisted of Cindy and Johan L. One of the climbers, Neil was an above the knee amputee. He lost his leg a few years before as result of a shark attack, and he was climbing with us to prove how effective a new technology in prosthetic legs is.

Things were extremely tense and rushed over the last couple of days. It is weird how people lost focus on the end goal when free clothing and equipment was available on a trip of this high profile. That meant it was a great relief to board the plane on the night of 8th October, 2007, albeit there seemed to be a lot of built up tension amongst the other members of the climbing party.

As the plane took off from Johannesburg the reality dawned on me that I had 'been there, done that' got the T-shirt' and was envious of the excitement building up within the rest of the climbing party.

I occupied myself with going through the everyday planning in my head and knew the notion to get to Simba Camp by the end of the first day would be pushing it (literally), failing this, would put us way behind my seven day plan. It was a goal to aim at though.

The flight was long and tedious, our first stop was Dar-es-Salaam then Zanzibar, which I must add was absolutely beautiful but Arusha was the destination and calling.

Deo, my lifesaver

We landed in Arusha at approximately 21.00hrs and the baggage collection went off without a hitch. Johan went outside to find the guides and we were greeted by five smiling faces. Deo, the head guide introduced himself and took charge of the luggage.

The bus journey was very bumpy, taking all in all about two hours but it gave the rest of the party time to satisfy their curiosity asking the guides countless questions about Tanzania and Kilimanjaro, the weather and the usual 'tourist' enquiries.

My concerns were discussing the logistics of the climb and finding out about the porters from Deo.

The trip took us through a shanty town constructed of very rusty corrugated iron sheeting, plastic bags and cardboard boxes, very little brick and water could be seen.

We veered off down a dirt road and there before us was this enormous gate which opened up into an awesome hotel complex. It consisted of a central boma for entertainment and meals, with outlying 'roundarvels' for accommodation.

Leaving the rest of the team to unload the luggage and find their respective rooms, I took Deo and Jacob, (Deo's

2nd in charge) into the bar area to discuss final preparations for the climb. They were very friendly and seemed well organized which was comforting as I had always used ZARA another guide company for the previous climbs. All bases had been covered, right down to the suggestion of taking wooden planks along with us for easier access through difficult places.

The rest of the evening was spent relaxing and the group asking numerous questions, Paul describing in detail the technology, website and tracking devices.

As we prepared to retire for the night, I stipulated how important it was to have an early start due to the distance we had to travel on the first day, I had planned on covering more distance that I had previous accomplished.

I got to know Johan a lot better through personal discussions and realized that he was definitely a person that you would want behind you. I had doubts within myself, but he filled me with confidence.

Gate to Forest Camp

The bus and luggage was loaded by 5.30am and we were on our way again, I was pleased at how everything was running so smoothly. The trip around the mountain would take us approximately four and a half hours to the main entrance gate. An hour into the trip we got our first glimpse of the mountain and I could see the rest of the group stare in absolute awe at the sheer size of the mountain. We could not resist asking the bus driver to stop so we could get some spectacular photos.

Registration, which should have taken a mere 10 minutes ended up taking two hours due to a problem with the payment system and to add to my frustration, I had requested that the climb be pre-registered, obviously this had not been carried out. With time ticking away I started stressing about the importance of adhering to the very strict time table we had to follow.

A constant stream of text messages between Jen and me kept my spirits up, I personally think if t was not for this I would have burst into tears in sheer frustration.

Registration finally completed, we had to re-plan where we would reach by the end of the first day.

We reached Rongai Gate at approximately noon, delays adding to my irritation I organized to take one of the guides and Johan with me and press on ahead, leaving the rest of the group to unload the equipment and they could catch up with us later.

As with my previous two climbs, the first 15 minutes was difficult to get into the rhythm but once I gained momentum, picked up the pace and made up on precious lost time.

Two hours into the climb we met up with a group of Americans also on their ascent who were absolutely stunned at what we were achieving, or planning on achieving. Although it was distracting, it added to the excitement and the group was in high spirits. With tongue in cheek I offered the Americans a wheel chair as they have had a greater success rate summiting Kilimanjaro than able bodied people. They joined us for about half an hour then carried on to their overnight camp.

On their departure, I was filled with renewed excitement and eager to get to Simba Camp that night but the realization also hit me that my aspirations may be a bit high.

Four hours into the climb from the main gate the same language barrier problems cropped up with the porters and me when I enquired how far it was to the rain forest, I was informed it was "just around the corner." Soon after I bumped into an old friend of mine Chombo, the main guide from my previous climbs and after a brief discussion with him, he suggested that pushing as far as Simba Camp was out of the question as my pace was too slow. For once, I had to agree with him.

Six in the evening saw us entering the rain forest and into the now familiar campsite, there we found Paul and Johan K waiting for us, although they were supposed to be part of the group from the beginning, they had decided otherwise but this was a sign of things to come.

The first night bought back the familiar feelings of 'being home' on the mountain but I was also missing my good friend Chester who had accompanied me on the previous two climbs. I think it was his confidence, leader-ship and his ability to organize the guides without a hitch that was the 'calling'. Tension was in the air and there was a definite sense of separation between Paul, Johan K and myself in camp that night

Leaving the Gate with team in place

Forest Camp to Past Simba

Our plan to leave at 6.00am the second morning was not panning out as Nadia was more interested in learning Swahili from the porters than getting herself into gear, causing yet more delays but Cindy and Johan came to my aid and calmed me down, suggested I write it off and put it down to youthful excitement. My anger inspired me to push the heck out of the chair and put trivial irritations behind me.

I often say that at different times, people need different mechanisms to get themselves motivated and although anger is not a lasting solution, it served to kick start my day.

Pushing and venting my frustrations out on my wheel chair caused me to accidentally bend one of the bars so it was dragging on the wheel every time I pushed down, this caused yet more delays as we had to bend it straight again. I guess it was a case of not knowing my own strength.

We had put an agreement in place prior to our departure that Cindy and Nadia would be with me but for the first two hours they lagged behind involved in conversation with the porters. Deo told me to let it ride and his team would accompany me, letting Cindy and Nadia enjoy the experience.

Good time was made through the rain forest; the path had been maintained and was not nearly as rough as previously, for me, it was like pushing over a smooth dirt road.

About three hours into the climb we were through the rain forest but the heavens opened, pushing my Kili chair through the rain was a brand new experience for me, and I might add, very interesting. The rain jackets were incredibly warm and with the energy I was exerting, I almost over heated.

It was becoming painfully obvious that we were only going to get just past Simba Camp that evening. I told Deo that I wanted to get at least fours pushing past Simba as I knew in this area we would be able to camp on the side of the path, we had done this before.

By lunch time, we were all in high spirits, I did a satellite video feed-back to the web-site and we were on our way again. Not long after this, things started going wrong.

Deo estimated how far we would get in four hours so sent the porters ahead to set up camp. Unfortunately, although my pace was impressive, better than I had ever expected, by 18.00hrs I still had not reached the camp site and was becoming irritated as it appeared that my record attempt might be in jeopardy due to bad planning. To set the record, I would be allowed assistance of up to 10% of the whole ascent, which equates to 2.7kms and needed to keep some of this in reserve for the summit.

Pushing past Simba Camp

By 18.30hrs I had sent everyone ahead, bar Nadia to find out where camp had been set up and was expecting Johan K to return with a report but Deo and his group returned to inform me that they would be pushing me the rest of the way as camp was still quite a distance and the likelihood of me reaching it by nightfall was slim and the risk of hypothermia was high.

I refused to accept this as I was still on smooth ground that I could conquer under my own steam and to waste any of the 10% assistance would be pointless just because someone had not been thorough with their planning.

All in all they ended up pushing me about 500 meters, every meter fueling my irritation as I was well aware that the climb the following day to Second Cave was going to be a long and hard one and it was my intention to use some of my allocation then.

Upon arrival in camp, extremely irritated and exhausted, but immensely proud of the fact that I had managed to cover just over 8kms on my second day. Everyone was a lot more relaxed that evening and in high spirits but I felt I had to warn them that from here on out the altitude would start having an effect on them.

Later that evening, to my elation I was able to communicate with Jen via text, although for a very brief period of time, it brightened my day considerably.

In the tent later that night, Johan and I discussed the events of the day and although it had not gone exactly according to plan and we had wasted some of the allocated assistance, it meant I was in for a much harder day three.

Past Simba to Second Cave

As day three dawned, we were greeted by the sight of being above the clouds that hung over Kenya, behind us was Mount Kibo, absolutely breath taking as snow covered it's slopes, so picturesque, adding to my excitement and awe inspiring.

My pace that morning was hampered because every time I pushed downwards, I thought my stomach was going to work. The lighter side of it was I had to instruct Deo to keep a portable toilet very close to hand, after approximately half an hour of pushing, I shouted frantically to the porters to bring the toilet closer, not many people can say they have sat on a toilet looking over Kenya!

All the hours spent in gym and hard training became evident that day as I was able to push harder and faster than I had ever managed before.

At about 10.00 we were able to get cell phone signal and

relay our location back to South Africa for the website.

It was also the first day that I felt truly content with myself in terms of the fact that I was going to achieve the summit this time. However, at lunch time it became evident that we would not make Third Cave that evening but would get as close as feasibly possible to it.

The terrain became very rocky which was great fun but we had to decide whether I should be assisted over this area as I had been in previous years or whether I should push to see how far I could go. Over these rocky patches I felt like a man possessed in terms of shouting and screaming, giving the motivation to push myself harder, a few times, nearly pushing myself right out of the wheel chair.

Not far from Second Cave it started to rain heavily, this was ironic as two years previously I had sat on a rock, pouring my eyes out on National Television as I had had to call it 'quits' for the day.

The going got harder over this rocky patch and with the rain causing rivulets and turning the soil to mud, my wheels began to spin, I ended up one big muddy mess.

The terrain deteriorated further up and I had to be assisted over large rocks as the passage through them was too narrow for the wheelchair. At around 14.00hrs with only approximately 100 meters to go to Second Cave, I had a brief chat with Deo and we decided to call it a day, largely due to the treacherous terrain and the rain that was intensifying.

When I got to camp and saw Paul, Johan K and Neil and told them that we would not be going any further that day they were very concerned that I was falling behind schedule but when I explained that we had to push further the following day and get past Third Cave they seemed to be OK with it.

Upon arrival in camp, Paul, Neil and Johan K expressed their concern that I was falling behind schedule, I explained that we would not be pushing any further that day but tomorrow we would push harder and get past Third Cave. This was acceptable to them but the tension was mounting rapidly.

Later on that day I could feel the tension in the group but my fears were confirmed when Deo and Jacob came to me and mentioned that they were a bit worried because they had just been approached by Paul and Johan K to split the group so that the two of them could go ahead and summit without the rest of the group. I explained to Deo that this was not an option as the group was to stay together at all times. The whole purpose of those three being on the climb was to video document my summit and by them splitting it would be pointless ever having them on the climb. The guides voiced their concern because I was the client and so they had to follow my requests.

I called the three of them into my tent and explained the sole purpose of them being on the climb was for them to be filming the event, not for them to go ahead and summit on their own as this was defeating the object of the entire trip, I thought this would have put the matter to rest. For the rest of the afternoon we sat there discussing how everybody was feeling and I once again had to explain to Paul and Johan K to slow down because they were already suffering from signs of altitude sickness. I am not sure whether my advice ever sunk in and this proved correct a while later.

We also got the first readings of the text line that was on the web-site, it was kind of nice for me to see how much support we were getting from back home. This was the night we started going to bed early because once the sun went down it got quite cold so there was nothing else to do other than just lie in your sleeping bag.

Second Cave to Past Third Cave

We were greeted by an amazing sunrise in the morning and it was nice to sit and have breakfast looking down at the clouds but the one thing that I do remember is that this was now going into the second day of having no cell phone communication with the outside world so I felt kind of lonely.

At around 06.00am, we sat where ever there was available space having our breakfast which consisted of some very dubious looking runny slop and the usual eggs which we were served every day.

Looking down at the clouds, my mind wandered to the fact that this would be the second day of having no cell phone signal and I felt a wave of loneliness wash over me but I had to focus on what was required of me that day because of time we had lost the previous afternoon.

I knew that the first section of day four would require the porters to carry me over an extremely rocky and unconquerable section for the wheelchair to pass through. I had planned for this section as it was one of the sections I knew ahead of time I would need assistance on but I was dying to get back into the wheelchair and push. But by the time we reached the beginning of the saddle I was itching to take my frustrations out on the wheelchair.

As with all mountain paths, the path was extremely narrow so I was forced to use the bushy sections on either side of the track which caused me to lose my balance but once I got into the rhythm of it my mood picked up and therefore my pace. As we got higher it became easier to push as for a while the bushes got smaller. It was nice to be surrounded by the porters because they were supportive, although distracting at times.

As the weather closed in we reached the beginning of the Arctic Desert area, although not quite desert but filled with low bushes, it was very difficult to push through because the paths were very narrow at times. Eventually I sent Deo and Johan K ahead of me at all times to source a new path for me. Just before lunch time I started feeling very ill and I realized that it was because of the exertion as well as the fact I had not eaten properly in the morning. We were forced to stop for an earlier than scheduled lunch. It was here that I turned my cell phone on to discover signal and a few messages from home and because of the climbing party had become so tense it was nice to get supportive messages from people that really cared for me.

The afternoon session was a big breakthrough for me because I had planned that I would need to be carried over this section but I was so motivated that I just kept pushing, finding totally my own path up the mountain. This was important because in my mind I was buying back some of the assistance available to me that had been wasted on day two.

By the time we got to Third Cave I could feel that I was psychologically and physically drained and was not sure that I could continue as which is what was needed so although my mood was high due to what I had achieved that day I was very happy to take a break and replenish my reserves for an hour or so. A decision had to be made whether I would continue that day to a camp site between Third Cave and Kibo Hut but I was determined to push myself to the limits and beyond to show that I could still achieve the goals that I had set out for myself,

One of the things that got me up and going after our little break was the fact that there was no place to put tents up, and the terrain was perfect for pushing the wheelchair, the ground was hard and the mountain side barren so it would be easy to make up time because my pace could be a lot quicker.

I noted at this stage that Paul and Neil were battling with severe headaches and so suggested to Neil that he stick with me so that I could monitor his pace and get one of the guides to watch his progress.

Those couple of hours after the break seemed very long because the group was not really talking to each other and focused on just getting themselves to the next camp. I think I put too much emphasis in my own mind on this and didn't really concentrate on what I was doing. Even though we were covering bigger distances now than the first couple of days with the effects of altitude setting in we were finding it increasingly difficult to breathe and I am sure if a stranger had heard me breathe they would have laughed because I was purposely breathing very deeply so as to not feel the effects to such an extent.

As we did the last couple of hundred meters into camp the porters were very enthusiastic and singing a few Kilimanjaro songs as I think for the first time they realized that we were going to achieve this challenge.

Paul filmed the last couple of meters into camp as well as interviewing myself and a couple of the porters as to their feelings on the day.

Over coffee that afternoon Paul shared his experiences of chasing crows away from the solar blanket and how a short little run had affected him in terms of his breathing and exhaustion. Again myself and Deo reiterated that from here on out to summit people should do everything slowly to conserve their energy.

That night Neil refused to eat and although I told him that he had to eat as this was the effect of altitude sickness he went straight to bed and suffered the whole night from nausea. Needless to say, the next morning he was worse and after taking tablets for his nausea, they would not stay down. A decision had to be made as to whether he would continue or not. I think this scared him to the extent that he was able to force food into himself just so he would not be left behind. But this served to show the rest of the group how serious things were becoming and how important it was to keep up your appetite.

Past Third Cave to Kibo Hut

The pace at which people walked in the beginning of day five was markedly slower and I couldn't help having a smile on my face because this is what I had been saying to them for days, take it slowly, conserve your energy but it had fallen on deaf ears.

The saddle area is very boring to walk through as there is nothing to see, just barren rocky areas. However, this day would be a very important day on my trip as I was going to pass the sign that Rodney had made for my Dad four years earlier, although it took a couple of hours for us to find it, when we eventually did, I was overcome with emotion and almost fell out of the wheelchair trying to get to the sign quicker. When I reached it I was filled with a feeling of being incredibly close to my father and knowing that he would be with me for the rest of the trip. After seeing how emotional I became Deo and Jacob undertook to maintain the sign every time they climbed the mountain.

After having got over the emotion of seeing the sign I seemed to have renewed motivation to push further that day. I had to set myself little goals because this section got very boring as it wasn't too physically boring, just monotonous. I got a bit too complacent towards the tea

"Kili-on wheels" sign
made for me bv Rod in 2003 in honor of mv dad at 4200m

break at about 14.00hrs because I said that the porters could give me a rest and could push for 50 meters. Looking back I guess I was just a bit overwhelmed by the strain I had gone through and was close to tears so I asked them to assist me.

I think the break we had for tea did me the world of good because after that I could see Kibo Hut which was base camp and it filled me with new encouragement although my body was starting to play up with the effects of altitude. After stopping for a piece of dry bread and coffee we continued on to Kibo Hut which seemed so close but was still a good two hours away.

This section was made more difficult by the freezing wind that I was pushing into but I had to laugh when we got to a huge rock in the path that I was expecting everyone to carry me over but I realized how well I had taught them not to help me as they made me push onto the rock and over the other side by myself. I still find it amazing that I had a wheelchair on top of a rock when they are not designed to even climb stairs. But once I was on top of the rock I could hear the voices of the porters that were at Kibo Hut so it showed me how close I was,

I was greeted into Kibo with singing from the porters of my favourite Kilimanjaro song and I said to Cindy that I couldn't believe that I was here again. This is the first time I ever saw emotion from Cindy when she burst into tears telling me how proud she was that I had got this far. I told her that it was partly due to her amazing training methods that my fitness levels were so high to allow me to get where I was.

I wanted a few team photos taken and when enquiring where Paul was, I was informed that he was not feeling too well and had gone to sleep in his tent, unfortunately he was not present for this 'moment'. A while later while having coffee Johan K informed me that Paul was extremely ill, hallucinating and shivering uncontrollably. Nothing seemed to warm him up.

After a few minutes of trying to comfort him and calm him down it was decided that the safest thing to do was rush him down the mountain on a Kilimanjaro ambulance to a lower camp for him to acclimatize properly. A Kilimanjaro ambulance is basically a stretcher on wheels, maneuvered by three porters. When they got a few hundred meters from Kibo Camp I heard a message that Paul was feeling better and wanted to come back. I said to the porters that this was not possible and that he should go down to the next camp which was Horombo for the night so he could acclimatize. Johan K decided to go down with him as support.

For the rest of the evening the rest of the climbing party were very shaken up by what had happened especially Neil but once I sat with him and explained that everything would be OK he calmed down but the mood was very tense at dinner time. It was decided that as we only had to get to Hans Meyer Cave by the next evening we would only leave at 6.00am the next morning. But this is where for me the seriousness of the climb started.

That night we hardly slept with the excitement and the nervousness of what was to follow and the fact that 70% of people that make it this far only get to Gilman's Point before having to turn back due to illness so of course everybody was wondering what their chances were of summiting.

Kibo Hut to Hans Meyer Cave

That next morning the remainder of the team set out towards the summit with a great deal of excitement pointing out people they saw that were already coming down, having summated at day break and we were trying to point out where Hans Meyer Cave was in relation to the summit as this was where we were going to be spending the next night.

I found myself easily irritated by things around me. I think this was just nervousness setting in knowing that the last time I attempted this I only made it to Gilman's Point and the pressure of me performing had set in.

I will never forget stopping for lunch after one of the steepest sections of that day and literally sitting on the side of the mountain looking down at the second peak of Kilimanjaro called Mawenzi having coffee and being able to receive and send text messages.

I organized for Deo to send one of his porters down to Kibo that evening to bring back a case of cokes for us to enjoy as a treat the night before summiting.

We got to Williams Point which is an altitude of 5200meters and we stopped and celebrated as this had been the sight of the previous record before I broke it in

View of Mawenzi from Hans Meyer (5200m)

2003. Once we had reached that point, Cindy realized that I wasn't very focused so she offered me her MP3 player which happened to have my favourite music on it so for the next hour I listened to Def Leppard while pushing to the cave.

We reached Hans Meyer a bit exhausted at approximately 14.00hrs with just enough time to sit and relax and enjoy the scenery and the cokes that had been bought up from Kibo before the sun went over the mountains and it got the hardest night of their climb so far due to the lack of oxygen and the cold and the fact that the best thing to do would be to have an early dinner and climb into your tent.

I must admit that I did not get much sleep that night because I felt as if my heart was running a mile a minute trying to pop out of my chest. The only thing that got me through that without panicking was the fact that I had expected that to happen.

Hans Meyer Cave to Summit

I was almost relieved when we got woken up in the morning to have made it through the night with no major difficulties as on my previous climb this is where I had started becoming sick.

The climb out of the cave area was very slow due to the loose shale and the fact that we had to zigzag up the mountain because of the steepness but at least I knew that this was the last day of pushing.

Just after breakfast Deo mentioned that he was concerned about the look in my eyes and the fact that my eyes looked glazed even to the extent of assessing whether I could go any further. Of course I panicked and pretty much pleaded with Deo to let me continue and assess my eyes after the next hour or so. Thankfully for me when he reassessed the look on my face he decided that I could continue but looking back on the experience I realize now that I wasn't at all feeling well.

It was very slow progress to the rock faces to below Gilman's Point but we made it there by noon and from there on I had to be carried over the rocks to Gilman's Point. Looking back I was extremely dazed but too stubborn to realize that something was wrong and also to admit defeat.

We got to Gilman's Point and took a few photos but I was extremely weak and had to be held when I was sitting. For a section between Gilman's Point and Stella the porters decided to carry me as I still had some allocated assistance left to me.

When we stopped at Stella for afternoon tea at 14.00 I passed out unexpectedly for about half an hour everyone was very relieved when I woke up again and I would not let them entertain the thought of turning back now as we were so close and I decided to keep myself going by climbing back in the chair and pushing the rest of the way much to everyone's disgust, but I think if I had not done it I would have deteriorated even further.

Once we reached the final few hundred meters and the excitement grew about reaching the summit the thought of my Dad, my Mum and the people who were at home waiting for me kept me going. I was very relieved when we reached Uhuru Point and very proud of the other climbers that they made it to the summit. The fact that we did it in 6 ½ days was also amazing. We took photos with the team, the sponsor's banners and one of the last things I remember is enjoying the sensation of being carried down after a successful climb.

On the summit, Uhuru Point 5895m for the final time.

LIFE AFTER KILIMANJARO

The next thing that I can remember is waking up in a dirty public hospital, not being able to move at all and feeling very weak. The first couple of days was like a dream but what I have since found out is that the night after summit after going to sleep after dinner I felt very ill and wasn't able to breathe and it was decided at 4.00am to rush me down to Kibo but once they got to Kibo and realizing I wasn't recovering Deo and the other porters decided that they needed to rush me down totally off the mountain.

While lying in hospital in a daze the only things I can remember are a couple of the porters coming to visit me and checking that I was OK until on the third day a medical team arrived and said that I was going to be evacuated to

Kenya for better treatment but at the time I had no clothes, no cell phone, no money and I felt totally abandoned. I burst into tears with total panic being rushed to a strange country, not being able to tell people where I was or even being able to get reassurance that everything was going to be ok. I remember lying in the airplane as we flew to Nairobi totally panicking as I was alone and driving in an ambulance to the hospital once I got to Nairobi wondering if I would ever have my wheelchair or cell phone again.

That first night in the hospital in Kenya was filled with uncertainty and fear as to what had happened because I still could not move any of my limbs. I was taken to a private ward and the hospital staff seemed very friendly and I didn't get much sleep that night because I couldn't even turn over by myself and this feeling was very strange to me because I had always been so independent and it left me with a feeling of the thought if I lost the use of my limbs forever which is something I had always been terrified of.

Over the next three to four days I was subjected to various tests because the initial thought was that I had muscular dystrophy but thank goodness my Mum was there to give them the correct information. I gradually regained the movement of my legs and my only excitement on a daily basis was the daily phone calls from Jen to see how I was.

I got to the stage where all I wanted to be was be able to relax in my own bed and as soon as I had taken the last pipe out of me I was able to be discharged and flew back, very weak the next day to South Africa.

Life as I knew it changed drastically. Things that I had taken so long to learn to do over the years were now very difficult. Jen and I broke up soon after I got back as she thought I would never get back to what I was. Although that really broke me at the time, after awhile I had to pick myself up and go again. It took me six months to be strong enough to drive and get back to gym. What had happened was the coma and swelling of the brain had caused me to lose the neuro pathways that I had built up slowly during my life. Basically forcing my co-ordination back about 20 years.

Ever since coming back from my last Kilimanjaro climb it has been extremely frustrating as I don't have the physical capabilities that I had before the climb. Whenever I got frustrated about my new situation I was reminded of something I said on national television after my second climb.

'Part of being positive is being able to change plans as you go along and realizing that not everything goes along to a predetermined plan. It's how you deal with the change that makes all the difference. And this is the whole story behind this trip - the fact that everybody has got mountains to climb within themselves.'

Sometimes those mountains are mountains in our mind. Real life heroes are not the cardboard cut outs of fairy tale endings. They are molded out of disappointment and defeat and the knowledge that true triumph is about trying, whatever the result.

When I asked nowadays if I regret doing my last climb in line of the sacrifices I say "No, I loved having a wheelchair above the clouds and every second on the mountain. It allowed me to end off a chapter of my life on a positive note, but at the same time allowing me to move on to deeper and more meaningful priorities."

Life is

10% what happens to you

and

90% what you do about it!

www.ingramcontent.com/pod-product-compliance
Ingram Content Group UK Ltd.
Pitfield, Milton Keynes, MK11 3LW, UK
UKHW020228250726
13967UKWH00001B/250

9 781446 756454